MW01600150

GOOGLE CHROME COMPLETE GUIDE

Your A-Z guide book on how to setup, explore, and master your google chrome with helpful tips and tricks just like a pro

N. FEDERICK BOSS

COPYRIGHT

TABLE OF CONTENTS

CHAPTER ONE

INTRODUCTION

The Google Chrome browser is made by Google and offered as a free download for desktop and mobile devices. In this book, we will be discussing about the desktop version, but it's important to know about mobile to access data and sync devices as well.

This guide is focused at the fundamentals of Google Chrome and the advantages you get from it when you use its features well. It is meant for beginner who wants to explore what the world's most popular web browser is really about.

Chrome is equally the name of Google's desktop operating system. It is what you will find on Chromebooks, or you can even install it by yourself. But Chrome OS is totally different from the Chrome browser.

Contrary to the popular opinion, Google Chrome is not an open source. It is just a freeware,That is said, Google released the source code it made Chrome from as a total different open-source project called Chromium.

CHAPTER TWO

INSTALLING THE GOOGLE CHROME

The very first step, of course, is installing the latest version of Google Chrome on your Windows, Mac, or Linux computer. Google updates Chrome always, so to get to the latest version you keep updating.

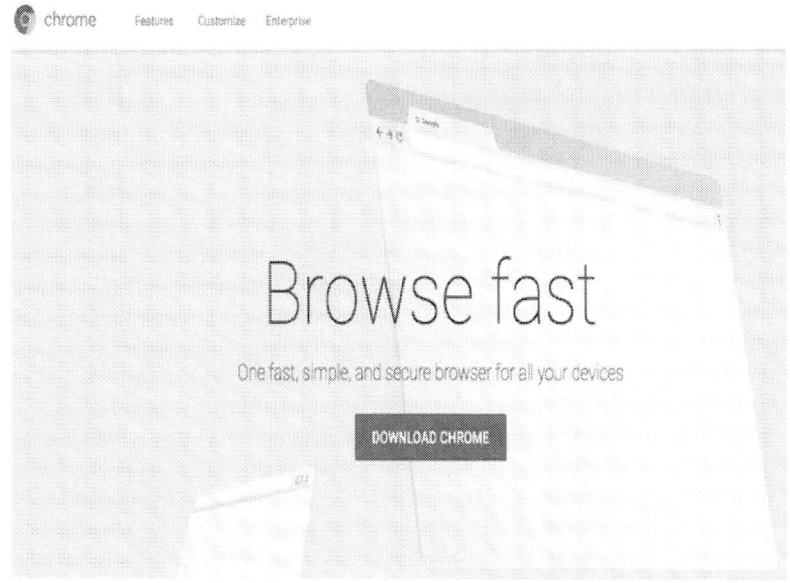

1. Go to www.google.com/chrome

2. Press the **Download Chrome** button

3. In the pop-up dialog that follows it, click **Accept and Install**

This will now start a file download. Immediately the file is downloaded, run it and kindly follow the instructions to install it. For any queries, simply refer to the installer's chrome home page.

Get the full Chrome installer for windows:

On Windows, the above method will download a small, partial installation file for you. You have to run it to start installation, in the process it downloads the full version of Chrome.

However, you can as well download the full version from the start. This full, offline installer is very easy if you don't want to download Chrome every time, or on any computer you wish to install it on. To eventually get this, go to the chromes offline installer mini-site and follow the same method as it is above. This time, you will now get the full installer, not the partial one.

CHAPTER THREE

SETTING UP YOUR GOOGLE CHROME

Before launching Google Chrome, you have to make sure you already have a Google account. If not, kindly create one at gmail.com.

When you run the Chrome, this is the first screen you will see. Then you sign in with your Google account.

As Chrome says, your bookmarks, history, passwords, and settings will all be synced to your Google account. Then, Chrome will have the exact data on your personal computer, office computer, and your tablet or phone.

You can now start using the browser:

You are now ready to start making use of the google Chrome. Let's now figure out the different elements of the web browser.

Tabs:

Tabs are the most vital part of a browser. Each of the tabs displays a link. Google chrome's tabs appear at the top of the browser.

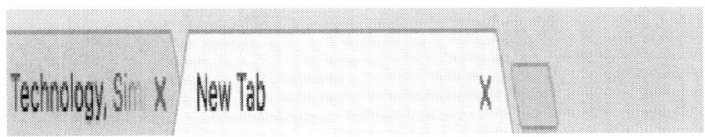

Now you can create a new tab by clicking the small icon next to the last tab. You can as well go to **Menu** > **New Tab** or you use the keyboard shortcut **Ctrl+T** or **Command+T**.

Omnibox:

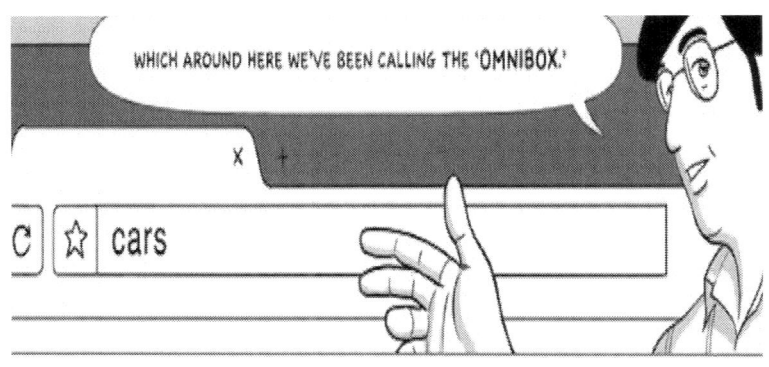

Under the tabs you will see a single bar, for both your searches and also to go to sites. It is called **the Omnibox.** By default, it uses Google Search, but you can easily change this in settings. You can as well type in a website address and click Enter to visit the site directly.

Menu:

Just next to the Omnibox, you will see the Menu icon. It is a three vertical dots. Press it to see the full Chrome Menu.

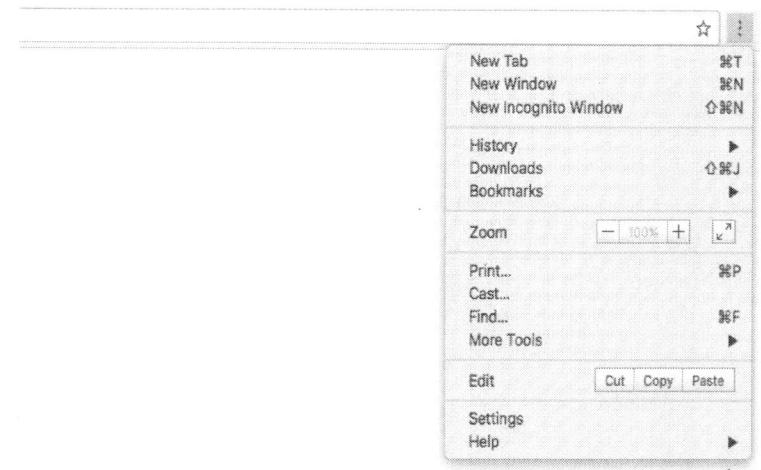

New Window:

You can equally have two separate Chrome windows running simultaneously. Each of the window will have their own set of tabs in it.

To start up a new window, you will go to the **Menu** > **New Window**. You can as well use the keyboard shortcut **Ctrl+N** or **Command+N**.

Starting up or New tab page:

Whenever you start Chrome or open a new tab, the default page looks just like this:

Having more than one page running at once will save you time reopening pages over and over again, and is very easy to do, just click on the new tab next to the tabs you already have opened, as shown in the image above.

Incognito Mode:

The Incognito Mode is an anonymous version of Chrome. It launches as separate window. The Incognito Mode does not have your Google account and doesn't save your passwords, history, or bookmarks as well.

You can simply launch an Incognito Window just by going to **Menu** > **New Incognito Window**. You can as well use the keyboard shortcut **Ctrl+Shift+N** or **Command+Shift+N**.

The aim is to have a browser that doesn't track you online. So an incognito window is a reliable way to protect your privacy and security. But be aware, it is not foolproof.

Bookmarks:

You can tell Chrome about your favorite pages and later access them without having to go through the search process again. Press the star icon in the search bar, which will turn yellow and provide a dropdown menu where you can choose whether to store the bookmark in a new or existing folder:

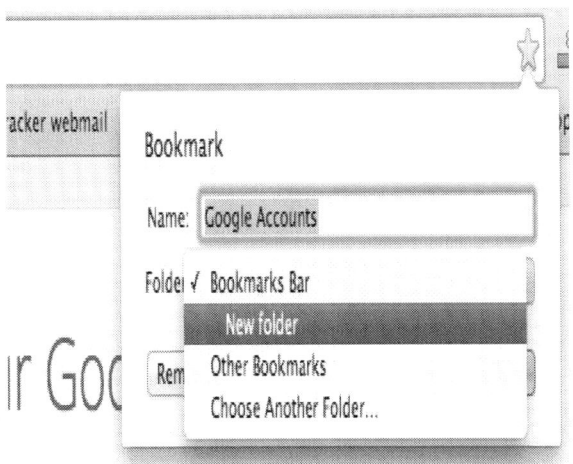

Dropdown list of Bookmark folders

To be able to access the page later, simply click on the Chrome menu at the top right-hand corner of your page.

If you want to bring up your list of bookmarks, click on the relevant link to open. Alternatively, you will have your bookmarks appear under the search/address bar by tapping the **Command Shift** and **B** keys simultaneously.

The amazing thing about bookmarks and other settings is that they can be synchronised to appear wherever you use google Chrome, whether on your laptop, mobile phone or tablet.

If you want your bookmarks synchronised, you will need a Google account if you don't already have one. Kindly go to **Create your Google Account**, follow the instructions therein, then, go back in Chrome, sign in by selecting **Sign in to Chrome** from the Chrome menu there.

Changing the search engine:

Many people make use of Google to search the web but this is by no means the only search engine. To try one of the others, simply click on the Chrome menu icon in the top righthand corner, then go to **Settings** in the menu that presents itself. Go to the section on **Search** in the **Settings** and click the Google dropdown menu.

Choose whichever search engine you like from the list given:

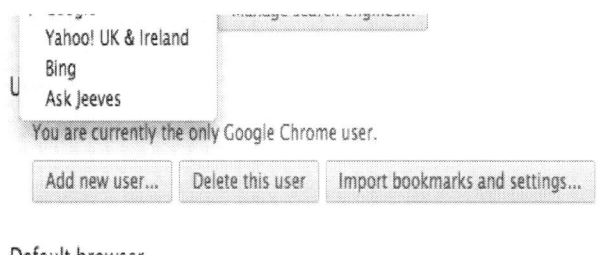

Your choice of search engines

The next time you make another search, it will eventually take place within your chosen search engine.

Closing a tab:

Having a lot of tabs open can be confusing and slow your computer down. To close an unwanted tab, just click on the little "x" in the corner of the tab.

Get on with searching:

Kindly take a look at Google, the default page that Chrome opens up with:

The Google search

This is Google search engine. Kindly type your search term into the top bar (or into the Google search field), as i did with *cats*:

Searching for *cats* either in Google or in the
search bar or at top of the page

If already you know the web address you need,
then simply type it into the top bar, for
example
twitter.com. The top bar doubles as a search
bar and an address bar for URLs as well (The
Uniform Resource Locators, or web page
addresses).

Here are search results for *cats* using Google
(it personalised some of my results for UK-
based sites, since I am based in the UK.)

Web   Images   Maps   Shopping   News   More ▾   Search tools

About 130,000,000 results (0.34 seconds)

Cats Protection - Caring for the UK's **Cats**: homing, neutering ...
www.**cats**.org.uk/ ▾
National charity which rescues and rehomes unwanted and abandoned **cats**, and seeks
to promote responsible **cat** ownership. Details of UK shelters, how to ...

Adopt a **cat** - **Cats** Protection
www.**cats**.org.uk/lewes/adopt-a-**cat** ▾
10+ items - Below are the **cats** in our care that are ready for homing.

Hazel.   Hazel is 5 months old beautiful kittie, a little nervous but will be ...
Touroux.   Touroux is about 6 years old and a love sponge, scared of male cats ...

Cat - Wikipedia, the free encyclopedia
en.wikipedia.org/wiki/**Cat** ▾
The domestic **cat** (Felis catus or Felis silvestris catus) is a small, usually furry,
domesticated, and carnivorous mammal. It is often called the housecat when kept ...
African wildcat - Creme Puff - Cats and humans - List of cat breeds

Cat
Animal

The domestic cat is a small,
domesticated, and carnivorou

Simply click on the link in which you are
interested to view the page.

To make a search within a page for a
particular piece of text, tap the **Command
F** keys on your keyboard simultaneously. This
will now open up a text box in the right-hand
corner of your screen where you can then
enter the text you want to find on the page.

Tap the **return** key and the relevant text is highlighted in yellow.

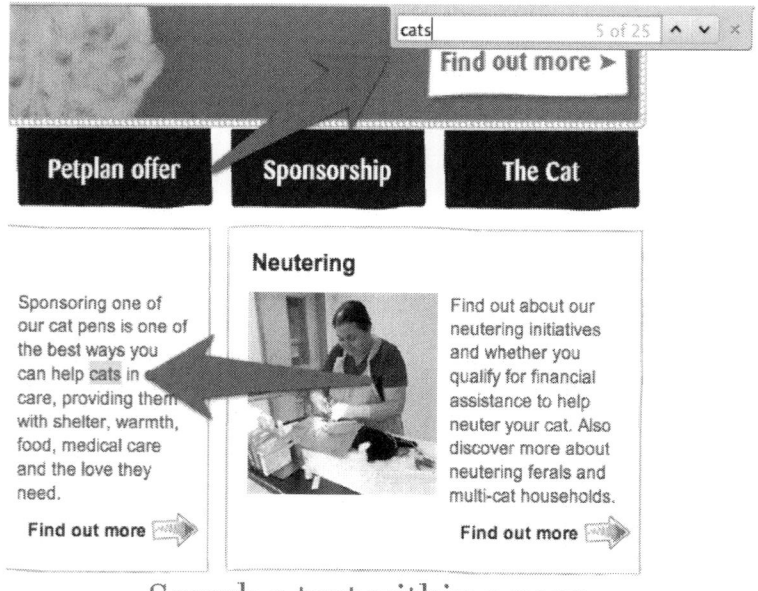

Search a text within a page
using **Command** and **F**

Viewing Search History:

If you want to visit a page you have visited previously but not saved as a bookmark, select **History** from Chrome menu. A page

appears where you can view the pages you
have visited.

Make your search by entering a keyword from
the site's name into the search box at the top
of the page.

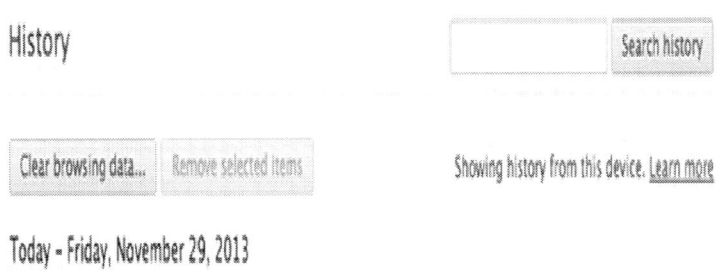

Enter keyword into the "Search history" box

Alternatively, choose **History** from the menu
that pops up on the top of your screen to see
the pages you have visited most recently.

Clearing the Search History:

While you are on the Search History page, you can clear any browsing data you wish to clear. Click on the **Clear browsing data** button (see the last image above) and simply select the data you would like to erase.

The Downloads:

The Downloads pane lists every file you have downloaded from the internet. You can bring it up through the **Menu** > **Downloads** or the keyboard
shortcut **Ctrl+J** or **Command+Shift+J**.

By default, Chrome makes use of the computer's designated default Downloads folder. You can also set up a custom folder in Chrome's settings.

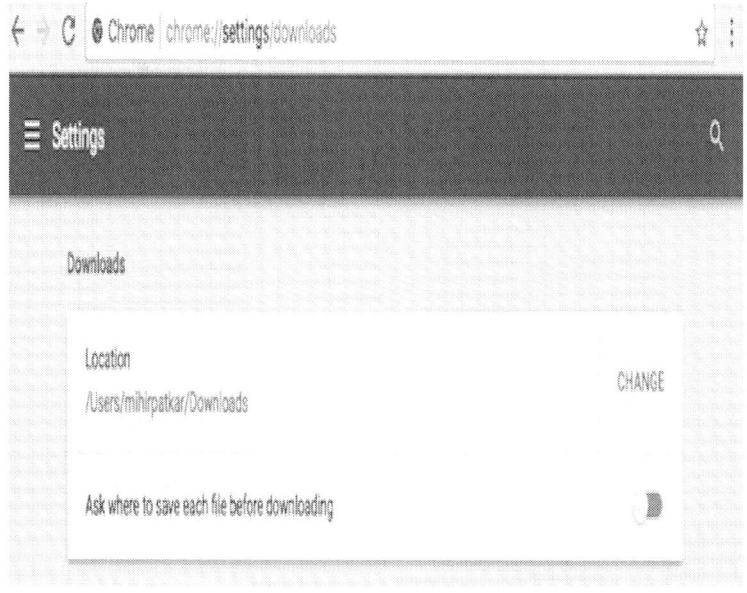

In the Omnibox, locate and go to "chrome://settings/downloads" (just without the quotes and without an HTTP prefix). Simply click **Change** in **Location** to set the folder of your choice. You can as well ask Chrome to ask where to save each of the file before downloading.

Guest Mode and People:

Just one Chrome installation can be used with other accounts, in case you share a computer or you have multiple Google accounts. In the top-right corner of your screen, above the Menu icon, you will see your name. Click it so it can reveal the People menu.

If you want to set up another account, simply go to **People** > **Manage People** > **Add Person**. Now choose an avatar (or you leave it blank to fetch your Google profile picture) and kindly sign in with your Google account.

If you want to hand over your computer to a friend, simply switch to **People** > **Guest**. Guest mode is a **blank profile for temporary use**. It does not save history,it can't use extensions, and can't access any information from the main user either.

CHAPTER FOUR

OPTIMIZING THE SETTINGS

You can access Chrome's Settings through the **Menu** > **Settings**. Here, you will be able to tweak almost any aspect of Chrome that you want. Here are few examples of what can be done.

1. Settings > Appearance: Here, you change the theme, then toggle the Home button and change the font and size of the font.

2. Settings > Search Engine: Select default search engine, and manage any search engines you can use. And you can as well create custom search engines.

3. Settings > Privacy and Security: Here you will activate "Do Not Track", protect from sites that are dangerous, clear browsing data.

4. Settings > Passwords and Forms: You have to save and manage passwords for websites, and add your personal information to fill forms quickly. But this is not safe and we recommend using the lastpass to secure your passwords properly.

5. Settings > System: Make use of a hardware acceleration when available, and set up a proxy.

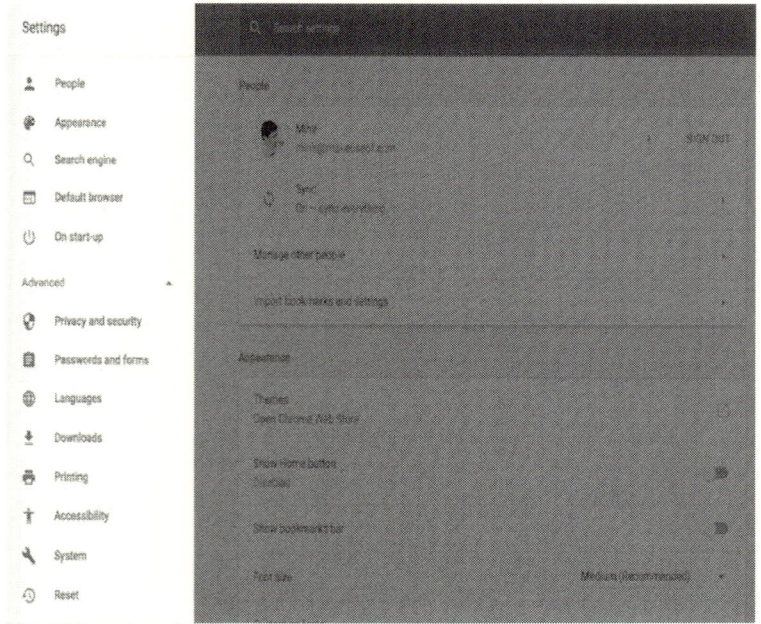

And you need not to worry about breaking anything. But in case you do, **Settings >**

Reset will take Chrome back to its default state.

CHAPTER FIVE

UNIVERSE OF CHROME EXTENSIONS

Extensions sets Chrome separate from all other browsers today. It has the largest library extension, that alone is enoughreason to use Chrome. There are few **exclusive Google-made extensions** that you should check out.

How to install a Chrome Extension:

Finding and installing an extension in Google Chrome is very simple. Chrome accepts only extensions from the Chrome Web Store and does not allow third-party extensions.

1. Go to Chrome web store

2. Browse or search for an extension, and tap on it.

3. Now you click the blue "Add To Chrome button".

4. Click on "Add Extension" when the popup asks you to.

How to manage Chrome Extensions:

Extension icons appears between the Omnibox and the menu icon. Simply left-click any icon to activate the extension. Press and hold, you have to drag the icon to change its position in the bar. You have to right-click any icon to see the extension's options.

The right-click menu also allows you to hide the icon in the chrome menu, or remove the extension totally. You can as well access the extensions pane by clicking on "Manage Extensions". The easier step, though, is going to "chrome://extensions" (without quotes).

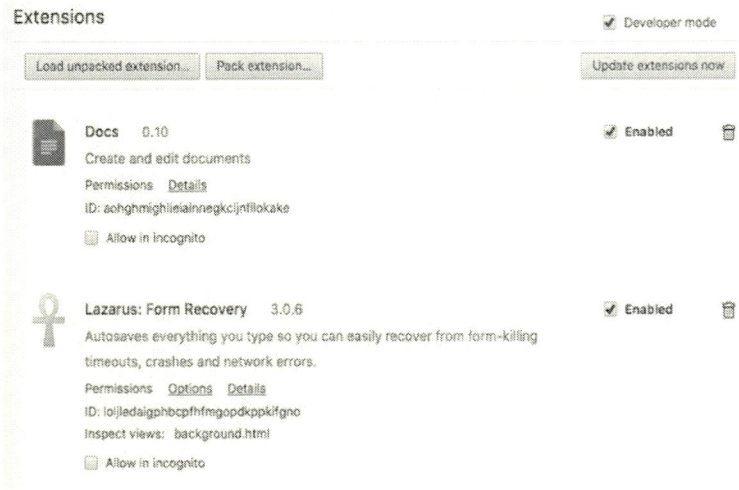

When you go to the Extensions tab, you will see all the add-ons you have installed. You can now enable or disable an extension, and remote it from Chrome, see what permissions it requires, and look up on other details. Some of the extensions offer advanced options, which you can access here anyway.

CHAPTER SIX

THE BEST CHROME FEATURES TO USE AND MASTER

Now that you have known everything in Chrome, it is now time to use it like a pro. There are few built-in features you need to master.

The Pin Tab:

You can "pin" tabs that you want to keep open with ease. The pinned tabs are moved to the start of the tabs bar, and shows only the site's favicon or logo. A pinned tab as well cannot be closed, you have to unpin it before that, this means you will not accidentally shut it.

To successfully pin a tab, you have to **right-click on a regular tab** and choose **Pin Tab**. Alternately, right-click the tab and then press **P**.

To successfully unpin a tab, simply **right-click on a pinned tab** and then choose **Unpin Tab**. Alternately, right-click the tab and then press **U**.

Reopening a Closed Tab:

Incase you accidentally closed a tab? You don't have to worry, you can reopen it. Chrome has the built-in mechanism to undo your mistakes.

To successfully reopen a closed tab, you have to **right-click on the tab bar** and then choose **Reopen Closed Tab**. You can as well use the keyboard shortcut **Ctrl+Shift+T** or the **Command+Shift+T**.

Chrome always remembers your browsing history in a session. So keep on pressing the shortcut and it will keep opening the tabs you closed, in a chronological order.

The Mute Tab:

Chrome shows you which tab is playing audio by adding a speaker icon to that tab. And you can easily mute or unmute that tab just by clicking the icon.

Alternately, you can as well **right-click the tab** and then choose **Mute Tab** or **Unmute Tab**.

You must be aware, this only mutes the tab, it does not pause or stop the audio. It is volume control, and not playback control.

The Task Manager:

Every tab and extension of the Chrome runs as a separate process. And Chrome includes a built-in task manager to find out which process is taking up too many resources.

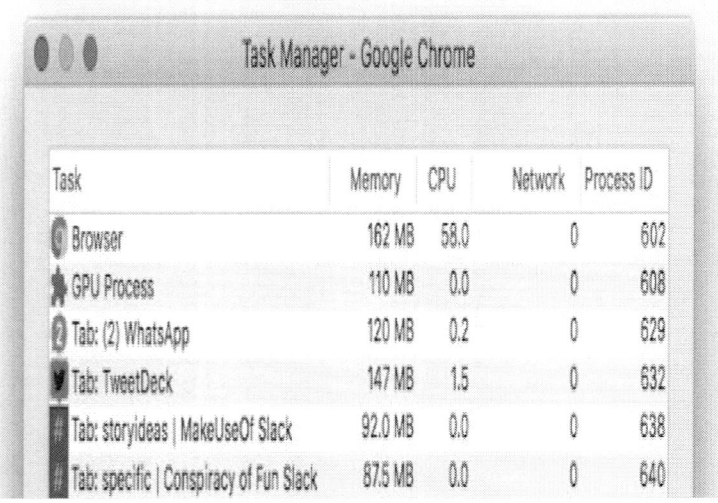

Task	Memory	CPU	Network	Process ID
Browser	162 MB	58.0	0	602
GPU Process	110 MB	0.0	0	608
Tab: (2) WhatsApp	120 MB	0.2	0	629
Tab: TweetDeck	147 MB	1.5	0	632
Tab: storyideas | MakeUseOf Slack	92.0 MB	0.0	0	638
Tab: specific | Conspiracy of Fun Slack	87.5 MB	0.0	0	640

The Chrome Task Manager shows you all the running processes, and how much memory or CPU has being used. It as well shows you how much network bandwidth any process is consuming.

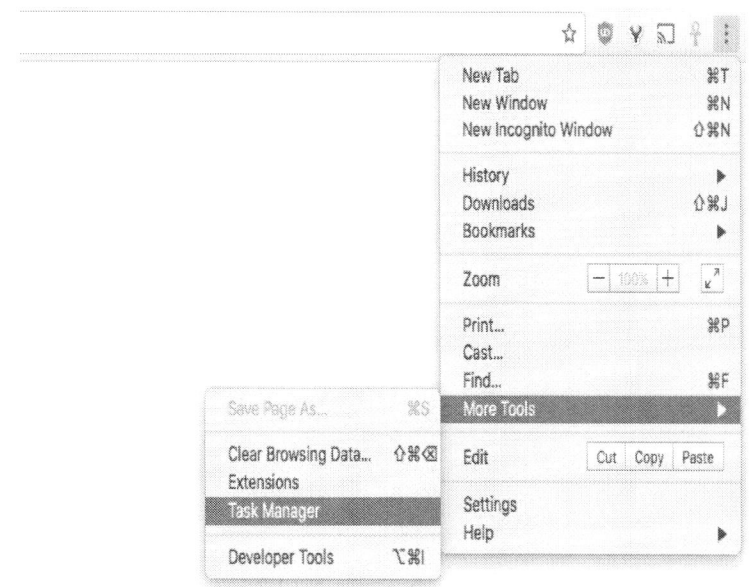

When you want to start Task Manager, go to the **Menu** > **More Tools** > **Task Manager**. On the Windows, Linux, and Chrome OS, you can as well use the shortcut **Shift+Esc**. There isn't keyboard shortcut for Mac.

CHAPTER SEVEN

THE CHROME HAS BUILT-IN CHROMECAST

The Google Chrome is the only browser that supports **Chromecast** out of the box. However, Chromecast extensions on the other browsers have not worked quite well for us whenever we tried.

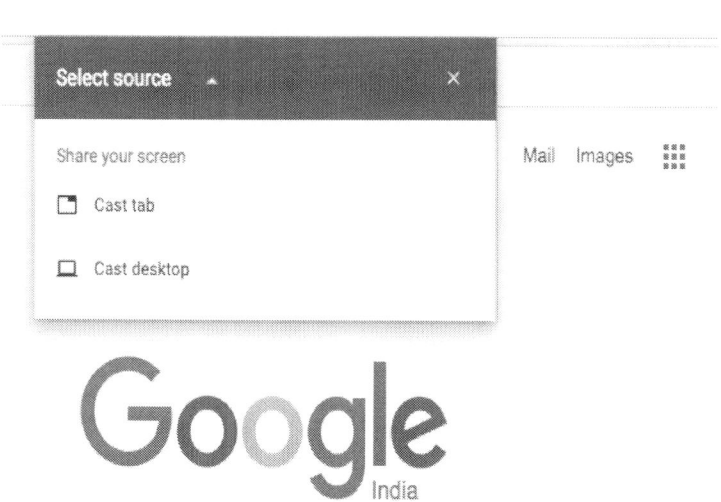

Chrome allows you to cast a video you are watching on a Chromecast-supported site, like YouTube or Netflix. You can equally cast the entire tab to your TV, or you cast your entire computer screen.

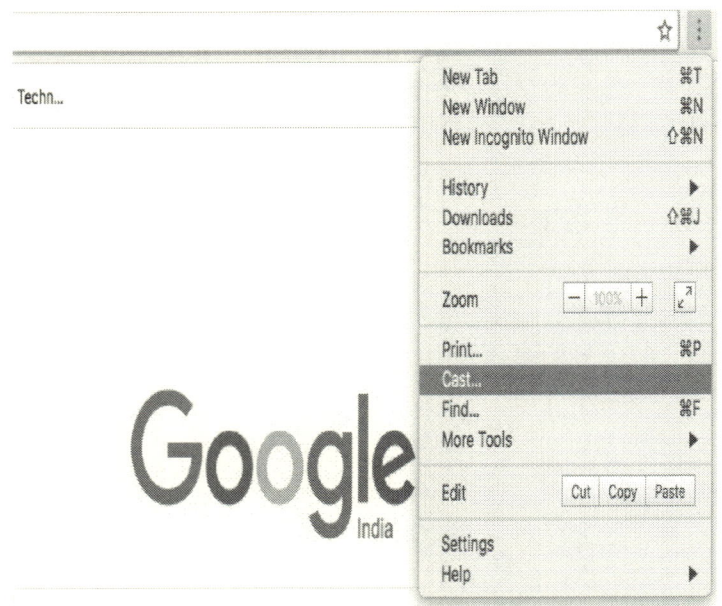

When you want to activate Chromecast, simply **click the Cast icon** next to the Omnibox, or you go to the **Menu** > **Cast**. The Cast pop-up will ask you to choose the device to cast to.

Kindly click the dropdown arrow to choose whether to cast a tab, a video, or your whole desktop.

CHAPTER EIGHT

MASTERING KEYBOARD SHORTCUTS FOR SPEED

Like any other good app, Chrome has lots of shortcuts for keyboard warriors. It would be too long an article to list each of them here, so here are some of the **more vital ones.**

Home: Scroll to top of the page.

End: Scroll to bottom of the page.

F5: Refresh current tab.

Alt + F5: Refresh all the open tabs.

Alt + Left: Go to previous page.

Alt + Right: Go to the next page.

Ctrl + D: Bookmark current page.

Ctrl + F: Search for a text on the current page.

Ctrl + J: Open Downloads manager.

Ctrl + T: Open a new tab.

Ctrl + W: Close current tab.

Ctrl + Shift + T: Reopen the very last closed tab.

Ctrl + Shift + N: Open new Incognito Window.

Ctrl + Shift + Delete: Clear the history, cache, downloads, cookies, passwords, and other data.

Shift + Escape: Open built-in Task Manager.

CHAPTER NINE

THE DIFFERENCE BETWEEN CHROME AND CHROMIUM

Chrome is a Google's end-product browser, which is complete with Google tools and services. While **Chromium** is the open-source code that Chrome is actually based on. Chromium is equally the name of the browser that is made with that open-source code.

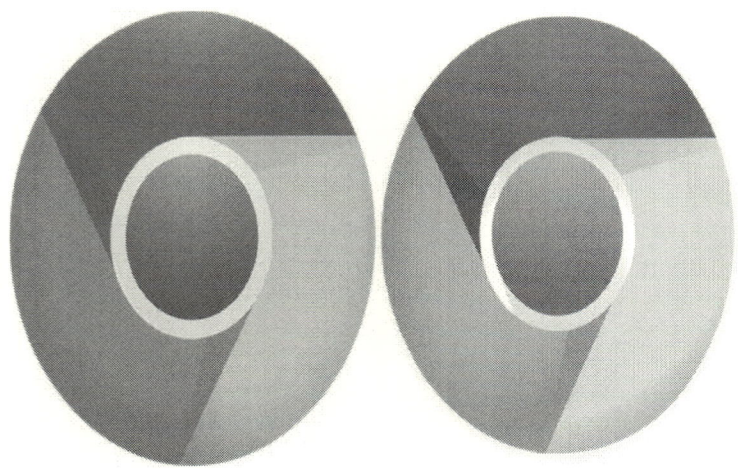

In a nutshell, Google took Chromium and they added more features to it to make Chrome. For example, Google loaded the proprietary codecs like MP3 and H.264, also added Flash, and has Google features like the **Translate** and PDF viewer. With the Chromium, you will need to add all those plug-ins manually.

But all the things considered, the difference is just minor. You can easily use Chromium instead of Chrome without ever realizing the difference anyway.

CHAPTER TEN

THE ADVANTAGES OF CHROME

So what has made so many people to use Chrome instead of other browsers? There are a few advantages that makesChrome outstanding from the rest.

Speed and Performance: In our comprehensive comparison of popular browsers, Chrome was objectively and without doubt the fastest. True to form, Chrome is as well primed for new web technologies like HTML5.

Fast Startup: Whenever you click on the browser icon, the Chrome browser starts almost immediately. With other browsers, you will likely have to wait for some seconds.

Security: Chrome treats each of the tab as a separate process so that a crash in one tab won't bring down the whole browser. Plus, whole of the browser is sandboxed, so malware cannot affect your computer only if you actively click on it.

Extensions: Since it is the biggest browser, developers like to make extensions for their Chrome. And that has led to massive extension library, which can nearly add any feature you want.

The Google Advantage:

Since it is made by Google, Chrome offers you a few Google features that make it great. Having access to these Google services as part of the built-in browser experience is a comfort that is quite hard to explain.

Chromecast: If you have got a Chromecast, then you should know that Google Chrome is the only browser to support it. You can cast a video you are watching, the entire browser window, or maybe your whole computer screen. This feature alone is enough reason to trap you forever in chrome.

Translate: Google Translate is awesome, but having it as part of the browser makes it more better. Whenever you visit a page that has a foreign language, Chrome will automatically translate the language for you. It is like magic.

Chrome Remote Desktop: Google has made free remote desktop application that works inside the Chrome. With this, you can access your PC from anywhere at all, as long as there is Chrome running on it.

CHAPTER ELEVEN

PROBLEMS WITH CHROME

Here, not everything is hunky-dory anyway. Although Chrome has so much to offer us, it is equally guilty of some missteps.

RAM and CPU Hog: This is the one problem that Chrome's developers have not been able to fix. The browser makes use of too much RAM and CPU resources, in the process bringing your computer down to a crawl. You will need to the chrome's Ram usage so you can free up memory.

Battery Drainer: Out of all browsers, Chrome consumes the highest amount of battery. Your laptop will definitely be out of power sooner if you use Chrome than Edge, Safari, or the Firefox.

Privacy Nightmare: Chrome publicly says it sends your usage data to the Google servers. And there maybe also some other personal data going with it as well.You should be concerned already about what the google know about you, and Chrome will only add to that.

However, do not let those problems bring you down. Definitely, there are ways to bypass them. Chrome is a customizable browser, and its arsenal of extensions will enable you make Chrome behave just the way you want it to.

THE END

Manufactured by Amazon.ca
Bolton, ON